HOW TO MAKE AWESOME COMICS

WITH

HELLO!

OOK!

PROFESSOR PANELS AND **ART MONKEY**

BY NEILL CAMERON

HOW TO MAKE AWESOME COMICS

is a

DAVID FICKLING BOOK

First published in Great Britain in 2014 by
David Fickling Books,
31 Beaumont Street,
Oxford, OX1 2NP

For Logan, Lex, Arthur, Lyra and Charlie. And also, for you.

www.davidficklingbooks.com

978-1-910200-03-2

1 3 5 7 9 10 8 6 4 2

DAVID FICKLING BOOKS Reg. No. 8340307

A CIP catalogue record for this book is available from the British Library.

Printed and bound in Great Britain by Polestar Stones.

David Fickling Books supports the Forest Stewardship Council (FSC), the leading international
forest certification organisation. All our titles that are printed on Greenpeace-approved
FSC-certified paper carry the FSC logo.

CONTENTS

I'M PROFESSOR *PANELS* – EMINENT AND WORLD-FAMOUS EXPERT ON ALL THINGS COMICS!

IN THIS BOOK I'M GOING TO TEACH YOU EVERYTHING YOU NEED TO KNOW TO CREATE YOUR VERY OWN *AWESOME COMICS!*

ALL YOU NEED IS:

1

YOUR (AWESOME) **BRAIN**

NOTE: DO NOT REMOVE FROM HEAD.

2

A **PENCIL**

(OR PEN.)

(WHATEVER, REALLY.)

3

SOME **BANANAS** FOR SUSTENANCE!

(OPTIONAL.)

...AND THAT'S IT, YOU'RE READY TO GO!

BY THE TIME WE GET TO THE END OF THIS BOOK, YOU WILL BE AN *EXPERT IN AWESOMOLOGY* AND A *COMICS-CREATING MASTER!*

DON'T BELIEVE ME? THERE'S ONLY ONE WAY TO FIND OUT...

"I DON'T KNOW HOW TO MAKE COMICS", I HEAR YOU SAY. "IT LOOKS HARD!" WELL, PISH POSH! I'M HERE TO SHOW YOU JUST HOW EASY - AND FUN - IT IS, IN...

CHAPTER 1

ANYONE CAN MAKE (AWESOME) COMICS

ART MONKEY CHALLENGE!

OOK!*

* OKAY, GUYS, IT'S YOUR TURN!

HERE'S A SIMPLE LITTLE COMIC STRIP STARRING TWO STICK PEOPLE.

BUT THE LAST PANEL'S BLANK - WHAT WILL HAPPEN? IT'S UP TO *YOU!*

'ELLO 'ELLO 'ELLO! IT'S THE FAMOUS CAT BURGLAR, 'FINGERS' JOHNSON!

OH NO, THE ROZZERS!

SWAG

YOU'RE NICKED, JOHNSON!

WAIT! I HAVE A SECRET! YOU SEE, I'M REALLY...

SWAG

BONUS CHALLENGE!

OOK!*

LEVEL 1 NICE AND EASY TO GET YOU STARTED! WE'VE LEFT THE LAST PANEL BLANK. WHAT HAPPENS NEXT? IT'S UP TO YOU!

STicK-MaN!

I SURE HOPE NO ONE'S GETTING UP TO ANY EVIL TODAY.

AIIIIEEEE! HELP! EVIL!

AH, NUTS.

WHAT'S CAUSING ALL THIS COMMOTION, CITIZENS?

RUN AWAY!

OH, MY GIDDY AUNT! IT'S...

NOW, A BIT HARDER. THIS TIME WE'VE JUST GIVEN YOU THE FIRST TWO PANELS!

"BUT I DON'T KNOW WHAT TO DRAW", I HEAR YOU CRY. "I HAVEN'T GOT ANY IDEAS!" WELL DON'T WORRY, BECAUSE I'M GOING TO SHOW YOU SOME EASY TIPS AND TRICKS FOR HAVING THEM, IN...

CHAPTER 2

HOW TO HAVE (AWESOME) IDEAS

HOW TO HAVE (AWESOME) IDEAS

SOME PEOPLE THINK THAT THE HARDEST PART OF MAKING COMICS IS HAVING IDEAS.

BUT HAVING IDEAS IS EASY! LOOK, I'VE EVEN BUILT A MACHINE TO DO IT!

FIRST, TAKE A BUNCH OF *STUFF THAT IS AWESOME.*

ROBOT **DINOSAUR**
WIZARD **PRINCESS**
cake **PIRATE** **GIANT**
NINJA **SPY**
schoolboy
schoolgirl **STUFF THAT IS AWESOME** **SAMURAI**
POP STAR **SUPERHERO**
DETECTIVE ...from the FUTURE
MONKEY ...underwater
JETPACK ...in SPACE!

THEN FEED THEM INTO MY PATENT-PENDING *AWESOME-O-TRON 3000!*

THEN: HOOK IT UP TO A *LIVE MONKEY!*

OOK?

THIS IS BASED ON A SCIENTIFIC LAW CALLED THE *PRINCIPLE OF THE MULTIPLICATION OF AWESOMENESS.*

(SEE? SCIENCE!)

THING THAT IS AWESOME + **THING THAT IS AWESOME** = **THING THAT IS TOTALLY SUPER AWESOME**

LET'S GIVE IT A TRY, SHALL WE?

OOK!

KID + DETECTIVE

= KID DETECTIVE!

GORILLA + SECRET AGENT

= SECRET AGENT GORILLA!

NINJA + DINOSAUR

= NINJA DINOSAUR

OH NO - THE MACHINE'S OVER-HEATING!

DINOSAUR + DETECTIVE JETPACK + BALLERINA CLOWN +++ ERROR +++

++ERROR++

++ERROR++
++ERROR++

BOOM

OKAY... MAYBE YOU CAN HAVE *TOO MUCH AWESOMENESS.*

ART MONKEY CHALLENGE!

 OOK!*

* OKAY, TIME TO CREATE YOUR OWN AWESOME NEW COMIC CHARACTER!

JUST USE THIS HANDY FORMULA AND AWAY YOU GO!

THING THAT IS AWESOME #1:

+

THING THAT IS AWESOME #2:

=

NEED SOME IDEAS? HOW ABOUT...

FIG. A: SOME THINGS THAT ARE AWESOME

PIRATE

ROBOT

DINOSAUR

NINJA

MERMAID

ALIEN

KID

MONKEY

APPENDIX ALERT

TURN TO PAGE 57+61

THERE ARE LOADS MORE CHARACTERS FOR YOU TO MIX UP IN APPENDIX A, PLUS SOME CRAZY PENGUINS IN APPENDIX F!

13

HOW TO HAVE (AWESOMER) IDEAS

IN THE LAST LESSON WE TALKED ABOUT CREATING IDEAS FOR COMICS USING MY PATENTED **AWESOMENESS PRINCIPLE!**

 +

=

THING THAT IS TOTALLY SUPER AWESOME

IN ITS SIMPLEST FORM THIS WORKS IN TERMS OF

– SMOOSHING TWO IDEAS TOGETHER TO MAKE A SINGLE CHARACTER!

GHOST ROBOT

GHOST ROBOT

 =

BUT YOU CAN MIX IDEAS TOGETHER IN ALL **SORTS** OF DIFFERENT WAYS!

FOR EXAMPLE, YOU CAN PUT THEM IN **OPPOSITION**

GHOST VS ROBOT

OR COMBINE THEM IN **ALLIANCE**

GHOST & ROBOT

OR YOU COULD EVEN PUT THEM TOGETHER IN **ATTRACTION**

GHOST ♥ ROBOT

OOK!*

* HERE ARE TWO BASIC CHARACTERS!

PUT THEM TOGETHER USING ONE OF THE COMBINATIONS PROF PANELS TALKED ABOUT, AND THEN TRY MAKING UP A STORY ABOUT THEM!

BARBARIAN

?

KITTEN

+

MIAOW!

VS

HO THERE, KITTEN!

I CHALLENGE THEE!

MIAOW?

&

COME, FRIEND KITTEN! LET US GO FORTH AND SOLVE MYSTERIES!

MIAOW!

♥

MIAOW!

AAH! BEGONE!

LESSON 5: HOW TO HAVE *AWESOMEST* IDEAS

 **ART MONKEY CHALLENGE!**

 OOK!*

*NOW IT'S YOUR TURN! WE'RE GOING TO TRY PUTTING TWO CONCEPTS TOGETHER AGAIN – BUT THIS TIME, USING THINGS PERSONAL TO YOU, TO TRY AND CREATE SOMETHING UNIQUELY AWESOME!

MY FAVOURITE THING IN THE WHOLE WORLD:

+

MY (SECOND) FAVOURITE THING IN THE WHOLE WORLD:

=

EXAMPLE:
(by Art Monkey)

MY FAVOURITE THING IN THE WHOLE WORLD:

BANANAS

+

MY (SECOND) FAVOURITE THING IN THE WHOLE WORLD:

BALLET

=

BANANARINA!

NOW YOU KNOW ALL ABOUT HOW TO HAVE GREAT IDEAS, I BET YOU WANT TO START TURNING THOSE IDEAS INTO AWESOME COMICS! FIRST, IT'S TIME FOR YOU ALL TO BECOME SUPER COMICS EXPERTS, WITH...

CHAPTER 3

HOW (AWESOME) COMICS WORK

NEE NAW

GET WELL SOON!

7:
HOW
(AWESOME)
COMICS
WORK

COMICS WORK BY SHOWING A SERIES OF PICTURES THAT, WHEN YOU READ THEM IN ORDER, TURN INTO A STORY!

EACH INDIVIDUAL PICTURE IS CALLED A **PANEL**, AND THE MAGIC OF COMICS IS ALL ABOUT WHAT HAPPENS WHEN YOU JUMP *BETWEEN* THE PANELS!

YOU CAN SHOW AN ACTION IN ONE PANEL LEADING DIRECTLY TO A REACTION IN THE NEXT!

BUT THAT'S NOT THE ONLY WAY YOU CAN TELL THE STORY. YOU *COULD* JUMP FORWARD IN TIME:

LATER:

OR YOU COULD JUMP *BACK* IN TIME, SHOWING WHAT HAPPENED EARLIER

EARLIER:

HEY! DON'T LITTER!

AH, WHAT DO I CARE?

YOU CAN CHANGE SCENE, TO SHOW WHAT'S HAPPENING SOMEWHERE ELSE...

MEANWHILE...

WHAT DO YOU *MEAN* YOU LOST THE EXPLODING ANTI-MATTER BANANA?

IF ANYONE STEPS ON THAT IT COULD *DESTROY* US ALL!

YOU CAN ZOOM IN AND SHOW THE DETAIL OF WHAT'S HAPPENING, TO SLOW DOWN THE ACTION AND BUILD TENSION...

OR ZOOM OUT, TO SHOW A WIDER VIEW OF THE SCENE...

TRY MIXING UP ALL THESE DIFFERENT WAYS OF JUMPING BETWEEN PANELS TO MAKE YOUR STORIES EXCITING!

BUT THE MOST *IMPORTANT* THING OF ALL, THE SECRET OF MAKING *TRULY AWESOME* COMICS, IS THIS...

ALWAYS REMEMBER TO...

WAAAAAAA!

OOK!*

* OKAY GUYS, YOUR TURN! HERE'S A COMIC STRIP WITH HALF THE PANELS LEFT BLANK! FILL THEM IN TO FINISH THE STORY, USING SOME OF THE TRICKS PROF P WAS TALKING ABOUT!

WE'RE GETTING A DISTRESS CALL - THERE'S BIG TROUBLE DOWNTOWN!

LOOKS LIKE A JOB FOR... THUMP-MAN!!

MEANWHILE:

WHAT'S THAT NOISE?

TEN YEARS LATER:

FINALLY, I SHALL HAVE MY REVENGE!

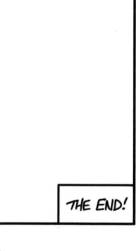

THE END!

ART MONKEY CHALLENGE!

OOK!*

* OKAY, GUYS, IT'S YOUR TURN!

TRY USING THESE THREE SIMPLE TECHNIQUES BASED ON THE PROF'S LESSON FOR SURE-FIRE FUNNINESS!

FUNNINESS TECHNIQUE 1

YOUR FAVOURITE ANIMAL:

$+$

THE JOB YOU'D LIKE TO DO WHEN YOU GROW UP:

BONUS TIP! Some common animals and how to DRAW them:

 CAT

 DOG

 MOUSE

NOW DRAW THAT ANIMAL DOING THAT JOB!

FUNNINESS TECHNIQUE 2

THE MOST SERIOUS, IMPORTANT JOB YOU CAN THINK OF:

$+$ A **DOOFUS**

BONUS TIP! How to draw *DOOFUSES!*

EYES POINTING IN SLIGHTLY DIFFERENT DIRECTIONS →

JAW HANGING OPEN →

GENERAL AIR OF GORMLESSNESS →

FUNNINESS TECHNIQUE 3

SOMEONE OR SOMETHING THAT IS **BIG:**

$+$

SOMEONE OR SOMETHING THAT IS **LITTLE:**

BONUS TIP! Some STUFF to have your characters GET HIT WITH

 FRYING PAN

 BAT

 LEMON MERINGUE PIE

 BRICK

 MING VASE

ART MONKEY ADVENTURES!

"MECHA MONKEY MELTDOWN!"

BONUS COMIC!

AMAZING NEWS, ART MONKEY!

AS YOU KNOW, MY *AWESOME-O-TRON* IS ALREADY CAPABLE OF AUTOMATICALLY GENERATING *AMAZING IDEAS* FOR COMICS!

BUT UNTIL NOW, TO ACTUALLY TURN THOSE IDEAS INTO REALITY WE'VE HAD TO RELY ON *COMICS ARTISTS.*

OOK.

AND AS WE ALL KNOW, COMICS ARTISTS ARE *FALLIBLE* AND *UNRELIABLE!*

AND OFTEN QUITE SMELLY.

OOK!

BUT NO LONGER! BEHOLD MY LATEST INVENTION... THE *MECHA MONKEY!*

BEEP-"OOK".

LOOK, I SIMPLY PLUG HIM INTO THE AWESOME-O-TRON AND HE WILL AUTOMATICALLY TURN ITS IDEAS INTO *AWESOME* COMICS!

LOOK, IT'S WORKING, HE'S DRAWING SOMETHING ALREADY! IT'S...

Sir Meows-a-Lot AND THE BANDITMOUSE IN: "All's Fayre"

WAK!

POW!

STOMP STOMP STOMP

FARRRT

IT WORKS! WELL DONE, MECHA MONKEY!

OOK!

25

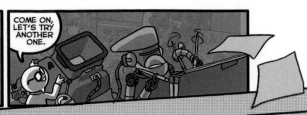

HOW TO DRAW
ANYTHING
(AWESOMELY)

HOW TO DRAW
ANYTHING*
(AWESOMELY)
*NO, REALLY!

AND NOW, WE'RE GOING TO TEACH YOU HOW TO DRAW ANYTHING!

VAMPIRES, NINJAS, MONSTERS, JELLYFISH... ANYTHING!

SEE, WHATEVER SORT OF CHARACTERS YOU'RE DRAWING, MOST ARE BASICALLY PERSON-SHAPED.

AND PERSON-SHAPES ARE EASY TO DRAW!

JUST DRAW A CIRCLE FOR THE HEAD...

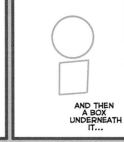

AND THEN A BOX UNDERNEATH IT...

...LITTLE BOXES FOR THE ARMS AND LEGS...

THEN DRAW AROUND THEM IN PEN AND...

TA-D...

THAT'S ALL THERE IS TO IT! YOU CAN MAKE YOUR CHARACTERS DO ANYTHING, WITH JUST THOSE SAME BASIC SHAPES!

RUNNING!

JUMPING!

SLIPPING ON A BANANA!

STUPID... PLACE... TO LEAVE A BANANA...

AND YOU CAN TURN THOSE SAME SHAPES INTO ANYTHING!

A PIRATE!

A ROBOT!

A PRINCESS!

A JELLYFISH!

UM... OKAY, JELLYFISH ARE A BIT DIFFEREN...

30

ART MONKEY CHALLENGE!

OOK!*

* OKAY GUYS, IT'S YOUR TURN!

TRY USING WHAT YOU'VE LEARNED TO DRAW OR TRACE OVER THESE BASIC FIGURES AND TURN THEM INTO CHARACTERS!

TRY ONE OF THE EXAMPLES FROM LESSON 10, INVENT YOUR OWN CHARACTERS, OR DRAW ONE FROM YOUR FAVOURITE COMIC!

APPENDIX ALERT

TURN TO PAGE 59

OF COURSE, THERE ARE SOME THINGS THAT AREN'T BASICALLY PERSON-SHAPED! SEE APPENDIX D FOR DINOSAURS!

HOW TO DRAW CARTOONS
(AWESOMELY)

AN IMPORTANT RULE TO REMEMBER IS *K.I.S.S.* THAT'S *KEEP IT SIMPLE, SIMIAN!*

FOR EXAMPLE, HERE IS A PICTURE OF A FACE. IT CONTAINS 347 LINES!

NOW HERE'S ANOTHER! IT CONTAINS 7 LINES.

THAT'S 1,200% MORE EFFICIENT!

THE KEY TO KEEPING IT SIMPLE IS TO FOCUS ON ONE OR TWO *KEY FEATURES* OF THE THING YOU'RE DRAWING THAT MAKE IT WHAT IT IS.

FOR EXAMPLE:

SEE? SIMPLIFIED DRAWINGS LIKE THIS ARE CALLED "CARTOONS", AND THE SKILL OF CREATING THEM IS CALLED "CARTOONING".

BY JUST SHOWING A COUPLE OF KEY FEATURES YOU CAN MAKE SURE YOUR PICTURES LOOK LIKE THE THINGS THEY'RE SUPPOSED TO BE, EVEN WITH REALLY SIMPLE DRAWINGS.

HERE ARE SOME EXAMPLES!

SPACEMAN — JET PACK, HELMET

WIZARD — POINTY HAT, WAND

WITCH — BROOM STICK

BURGLAR — MASK, SWAG BAG, SWAG

SPY — SHADES, GUN

DETECTIVE

NINJA — NINJA MASK

KNIGHT — SHIELD

PRINCESS — SWORD, TIARA

SUPERHERO — CAPE, PANTS

CHEF — BIG HAT, PAN

PROFESSOR — NERDY GLASSES, WHITE COAT

HEY!

ART MONKEY CHALLENGE!

OOK!*

* HERE IS A PIRATE ORANGUTAN!

THIS IS QUITE A DETAILED DRAWING. TRY DRAWING YOUR OWN, CARTOONIFIED VERSION!

JUST THINK ABOUT WHAT HIS KEY FEATURES ARE, AND TRY DRAWING A SUPER-SIMPLE VERSION OF THEM!

HOW TO DRAW (AWESOME) FACES

TIME TO TALK ABOUT *FACES!* WE'VE LOOKED AT HOW YOU CAN DRAW A FACE IN QUITE A DETAILED WAY...

OR MAKE IT SIMPLER:

BUT YOU CAN MAKE IT SIMPLER STILL...

...AND *EVEN* SIMPLER...

...TO THE POINT WHERE IT'S NOT A DRAWING ANY MORE AT *ALL!*

IT'S ALL ABOUT FOCUSING ON WHAT'S *ESSENTIAL* ABOUT AN EXPRESSION.

AS YOU MAKE IT SIMPLER YOU LOSE ALL THE NON-ESSENTIAL STUFF: HOW *OLD* THE CHARACTER IS, THEIR *WEIGHT*...

WHETHER THEY *SHAVED* THAT DAY...

...EVEN WHAT THEY LOOK LIKE AT *ALL*...

...UNTIL YOU'RE LEFT WITH JUST ONE THING...

THE *EMOTION!*

FOCUS ON WHAT'S HAPPENING IN *THREE KEY AREAS:*

- THE *EYES*
- THE *EYEBROWS*
- THE *MOUTH*

AND YOU CAN USE REALLY SIMPLE DRAWINGS TO SHOW A WHOLE *RANGE* OF EMOTIONS...

ANGRY

SURPRISED

WORRIED

PAINED

CRAZY

SMUG

CROSS

AMUSED

AFRAID

SLEEPY

SHOCKED

DEAD

COCKY

SUSPICIOUS

JUST DONE A FART

JUST SMELLED A FART

OOOK!*

*TIME FOR A SPECIAL ART MONKEY CHALLENGE!

HERE'S A COMIC STRIP I MADE EARLIER, BUT THERE'S ONE THING MISSING...

...THE FACES! IT'S UP TO YOU TO DRAW FACES ONTO THE TWO CHARACTERS!

TRY TO MAKE THEIR EXPRESSIONS MATCH WHAT THEY'RE SAYING!

OR DON'T! FACE IT - IT'S UP TO YOU!

ART MONKEY PRESENTS...

THEATRE... OF EMOTION!

STARRING:  AND

HEY, BUDDY! GOOD TO SEE YOU!

WELL IT'S NOT GOOD TO SEE YOU!

WHAT'S THE MATTER? DID I DO SOMETHING WRONG?

YOU FORGOT MY BIRTHDAY! NOW I AM SAD AND ANGRY!

I'M SORRY! I - EWWWWW!! HAVE YOU FARTED?

YES! HA HA HA HA HA HA HA!

FARTS.

HOW TO DRAW (AWESOME) ROBOTS

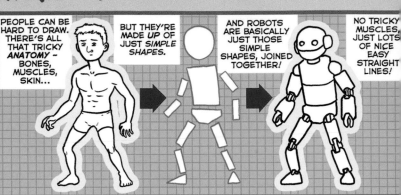

ROBOTS! NOT ONLY ARE ROBOTS ONE OF THE *MOST AWESOMEST THINGS OF ALL,* THEY ARE ALSO SUPER-EASY TO DRAW!

LET'S SEE!

PEOPLE CAN BE HARD TO DRAW. THERE'S ALL THAT TRICKY *ANATOMY* – BONES, MUSCLES, SKIN...

BUT THEY'RE MADE *UP* OF JUST *SIMPLE* SHAPES.

AND ROBOTS ARE BASICALLY JUST THOSE *SIMPLE* SHAPES, JOINED TOGETHER!

NO TRICKY MUSCLES, JUST LOTS OF NICE EASY STRAIGHT LINES!

ROBOTS AREN'T JUST HUMAN EITHER! YOU CAN TURN ANYTHING INTO SIMPLE SHAPES.

JUST FIND THE MOST *BASIC SHAPES* THAT MAKE SOMETHING UP...

THOSE SAME SHAPES WILL JOIN TOGETHER TO CREATE A *ROBOT!*

(...MAYBE ADD SOME *MISSILES,* FOR GOOD LUCK!)

(*EVERYONE* LOVES MISSILES!)

THE TRICK TO MAKING YOUR ROBOT LOOK AMAZING IS TO THINK ABOUT HOW THE SIMPLE SHAPES *JOIN TOGETHER!* THE DETAIL YOU PUT IN THE *JOINTS* WILL REALLY BRING YOUR ROBOT TO LIFE!

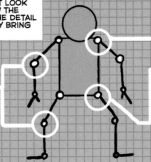

HINGED JOINTS (ELBOWS, KNEES) – MOVE IN ONE DIRECTION!

BALL + SOCKET JOINTS (E.G. SHOULDERS, HIPS) – MOVE IN ALL DIRECTIONS.

OR, HEY, THEY'RE *ROBOTS* – PUT SOME CRAZY ROBOT PIPES ON THERE!

APPENDIX ALERT
TURN TO PAGE 58

HAVE A LOOK AT APPENDIX B FOR LOADS OF COOL ACCESSORIES TO ADD TO YOUR ROBOTS!

EASY, RIGHT? JUST SIMPLE SHAPES WITH DETAILED JOINTS! (AND SOME MISSILES.)

ONCE YOU'VE GOT THE HANG OF THOSE BASICS, YOU CAN DRAW *ALL* DIFFERENT STYLES AND FLAVOURS OF ROBOT!

MANGA   **RETRO**   **RUSTY**

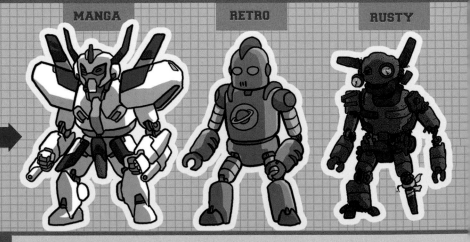

OOK!*

* TIME TO PUT THOSE ROBOT-DRAWING SKILLS INTO ACTION!

HERE'S A THRILLING ROBOTIC COMIC STRIP FOR YOU TO FINISH OFF!

USE THE BASIC SHAPES BELOW TO INVENT YOUR OWN ROBOT! THINK ABOUT THE JOINTS, DETAILS AND ACCESSORIES, AND WHAT STYLE IT WILL BE IN!

RUN FOR YOUR LIVES! IT'S...

-BOT!

AND HE'S DESTROYING THE CITY WITH HIS GIANT ROBOTIC   !

DOCTOR SCIENCE, ISN'T THERE ANYTHING THAT CAN DEFEAT THIS METAL MONSTER?

HMMM-IT'S A LONG SHOT, BUT IT JUST MIGHT WORK - MY LATEST INVENTION...

...THE   -CANNON!

TAKE THAT!

THANKS, DOC!

DON'T THANK ME. THANK SCIENCE!

HERE'S YOUR REWARD: !

HOW TO DRAW

(AWESOME) **Pirates**

SO, TO SUM UP: ONE OF THE MOST IMPORTANT PARTS OF CARTOONING IS *SIMPLIFYING*...

...STRIPPING OUT UNNECESSARY DETAILS...

...AND JUST FOCUSING ON WHAT'S ESSENTIAL!

BUT NOT ALL DETAIL *IS* UNNECESSARY. IT'S BY *ADDING* KEY DETAILS THAT YOU CAN REALLY GIVE YOUR CHARACTERS... WELL, CHARACTER!

WITH JUST A COUPLE OF LINES, YOU CAN MAKE YOUR CHARACTER LOOK OLDER...

GIVING THEM *LAUGHTER LINES*...

...AND *WRINKLES*...

UNTIL THEY LOOK ALL *OLD* AND *GNARLED!*

AND THAT'S JUST THE START! THEN THERE'S THE WHOLE EXCITING WORLD OF FACIAL HAIR: *MOUSTACHES*...

BEARDS...

SIDEBURNS...

...AND *CRAZY, OLD-DUDE EYEBROWS!*

NICELY *GNARLED!* NOW LET'S JUST ADD A FEW MORE KEY BITS OF FACIAL FURNITURE...

...UNTIL HE STARTS TO LOOK LIKE A PROPER, NAUTICAL...

...GRIZZLED, TOUGH-AS-NAILS, SALTY OLD...

...*PIRATE!*

ART MONKEY CHALLENGE!

 OOK!*

* HERE IS A NICE, FRIENDLY LOOKING FELLOW!

...NOW SEE HOW MESSED-UP, GNARLY AND PROPERLY PIRATEY YOU CAN MAKE HIM!

APPENDIX
TURN TO PAGE 58
ALERT

NEED SOME MORE INSPIRATION? CHECK OUT APPENDIX C FOR PIRATEY FACIAL HAIR!

REMEMBER MY PATENTED *AWESOMENESS PRINCIPLE* FROM CHAPTER 2? WELL OF COURSE YOU DO. IT'S *AWESOME*.

THING THAT IS AWESOME + THING THAT IS AWESOME = **THING THAT IS TOTALLY SUPER AWESOME**

e.g. wizard + bear = **WIZARD BEAR**

NOW, YOU MAY THINK THIS IS A NEW IDEA, BUT IN FACT IT'S SOMETHING THAT HUMANS HAVE BEEN USING SINCE...

...WELL, PRETTY MUCH SINCE THERE HAVE BEEN *HUMANS*!

EVER SINCE THE *DAWN OF TIME*, PEOPLE HAVE BEEN PUTTING TWO THINGS TOGETHER TO MAKE SOMETHING NEW...

= ?

...AND COMING UP WITH ALL *MANNER* OF FREAKY AND FANTASTICAL CREATURES!

MYTHS & LEGENDS

BONUS GAME!
CAN YOU NAME ALL THE MONSTERS IN THIS PICTURE?

TO MAKE YOUR MONSTERS LOOK COOL, TRY TAKING THE COOLEST OR THE *SCARIEST* PARTS OF DIFFERENT CREATURES...

CLAWS TEETH TENTACLES TAILS LEGS WINGS TUSKS EYEBALLS ANTENNAE

...AND MIXING THEM UP TO MAKE SOMETHING *NEW*!

...LIKE SO!

YIKES!

ART MONKEY CHALLENGE!

OOK!*

* MIX AND MATCH THE PARTS OF THESE ANIMALS TO MAKE A MONSTER! GIVE IT AN AWESOME MONSTER NAME! DRAW YOUR FAVOURITE ANIMAL IN THE BLANK SPACE TO ADD TO THE MIX!

APPENDIX ALERT

TURN TO PAGE **64**

ONCE YOU'VE MADE UP YOUR MONSTER, WHY NOT DRAW IT ON THE BONUS PIN-UP IN APPENDIX H?

BONUS GAME ANSWERS! GRIFFIN, SPHINX, CENTAUR, GORGON, MINOTAUR, TENGU.

SO, BY NOW YOU'VE GOT YOUR AWESOME IDEAS, AND YOU'RE READY TO START DRAWING THEM! BUT HOW DO YOU TURN THEM INTO ACTUAL STORIES? I'M GOING TO SHOW YOU SOME EASY WAYS TO DO JUST THAT! IT'S TIME FOR...

CHAPTER 5

HOW TO TELL (AWESOME) STORIES

LESSON 16: HOW TO TELL (AWESOME) STORIES

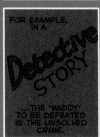

ART MONKEY CHALLENGE!

OOK!*

* DON'T WORRY, GUYS – THE PROF IS JUST WINDING YOU UP. HE KNOWS THERE ARE LOTS OF DIFFERENT WAYS TO TELL STORIES, REALLY!

...AT LEAST, I THINK HE DOES!

ANYWAY, IT'S TIME TO TRY IT YOURSELF – CHOOSE ONE OF YOUR OWN FAVOURITE STORIES – IT COULD BE A BOOK, A FILM, OR ONE OF THE STORIES IN THIS VERY COMIC – AND TRY CONDENSING THE STORY DOWN INTO A FOUR PANEL COMIC VERSION!

1. GOODY

2. BADDY

3. THEY HAVE A FIGHT

4. GOODY WINS

LESSON 17: HOW TO CREATE (AWESOME) HEROES

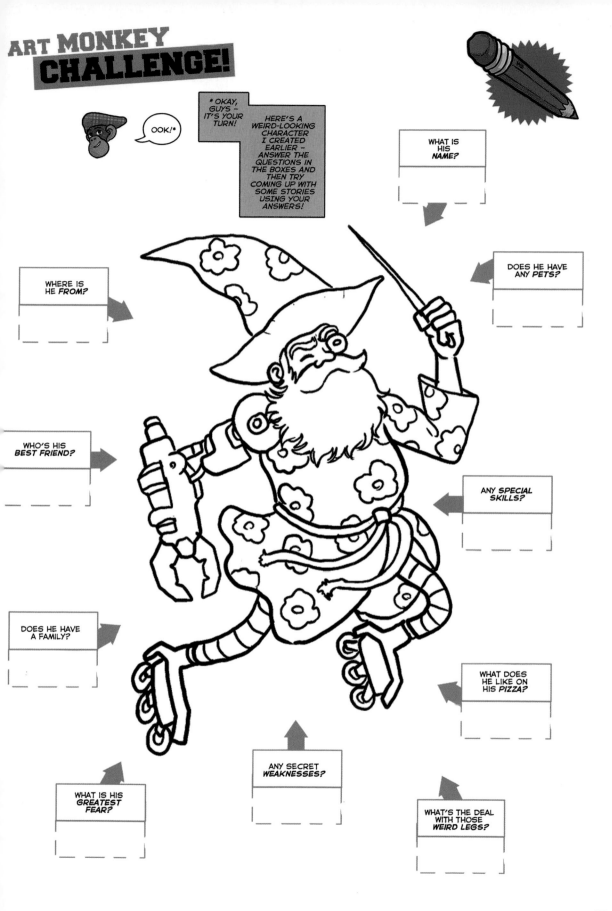

ART MONKEY CHALLENGE!

OOK!*

* OKAY, GUYS – IT'S YOUR TURN!

HERE'S A WEIRD-LOOKING CHARACTER I CREATED EARLIER – ANSWER THE QUESTIONS IN THE BOXES AND THEN TRY COMING UP WITH SOME STORIES USING YOUR ANSWERS!

WHAT IS HIS *NAME?*

DOES HE HAVE ANY *PETS?*

WHERE IS HE *FROM?*

WHO'S HIS *BEST FRIEND?*

ANY *SPECIAL SKILLS?*

DOES HE HAVE A FAMILY?

WHAT DOES HE LIKE ON HIS *PIZZA?*

WHAT IS HIS *GREATEST FEAR?*

ANY SECRET *WEAKNESSES?*

WHAT'S THE DEAL WITH THOSE *WEIRD LEGS?*

HOW TO CREATE (AWESOME) VILLAINS

SO NOW YOU KNOW ALL ABOUT HOW TO CREATE YOUR OWN AWESOME HEROES!

BUT WHAT DOES EVERY GOOD HERO NEED?

GOODY BADDY THEY FIGHT GOODY WINS

A VILLAIN! SOMEONE TO PLAGUE, PESTER AND CREATE PROBLEMS FOR THEM.

THE MADDER, CRAZIER AND CREEPIER THE BETTER!

TO COME UP WITH AN AWESOME VILLAIN, TRY THINKING ABOUT YOUR HERO'S OPPOSITES.

WHO IS YOUR HERO'S NATURAL ENEMY?

HERE ARE SOME EXAMPLES!

SUPER HERO	DETECTIVE	SPY	PRINCESS	PIRATE	ASTRONAUT
VS	VS	VS	VS	VS	VS
SUPER VILLAIN	CRIMINAL	EVIL MASTER-MIND	WICKED WITCH	NAVY	ALIEN

WHEN DESIGNING A VILLAIN, USE THINGS THAT ARE CREEPY, WEIRD, OR SCARY!

STUFF LIKE THIS!

GIANT BRAINS
SLIME
SPIDERS
SPIKES
BANK ROBBERS
SKULLS
STUFF THAT IS SCARY!
VAMPIRES
FIRE
ZOMBIES
MAD PROFESSORS
monsters
MUMMIES
CLOWNS
creepy crawlies
WEREWOLVES

...BUT MAYBE DON'T USE ALL OF THEM AT ONCE!

OOK!

ART MONKEY CHALLENGE!

OOK!*

* HERE IS A BRAND NEW HERO: THE INCREDIBLE...

SPACE VET

VS

USE THE PROF'S TIPS TO MAKE UP AN AWESOME NEW VILLAIN TO CAUSE PROBLEMS FOR HER!

APPENDIX

TURN TO PAGE 60

ALERT

NEED SOME INSPIRATION? FOR SOME CREEPY VILLAIN IDEAS CHECK OUT APPENDIX E!

19: CREATING (AWESOME) DRAMA

WE'VE TALKED ABOUT CREATING AWESOME HEROES AND VILLAINS, SO NOW IT'S TIME TO LOOK AT THE REAL MEAT OF YOUR STORY

...CONFLICT!

NOW, CONFLICT CAN TAKE ALL SORTS OF FORMS. FOR EXAMPLE...

PHYSICAL

I HIT YOU!

POW!

MENTAL

YOU MUST DEFEAT ME AT CHESS... ...OR DIE!

EMOTIONAL

YOU ATE MY COOKIE?!

UM, WELL...

BUT WHATEVER FORM THE CONFLICT TAKES, YOU WANT IT TO MATTER.

THE STAKES SHOULD BE REAL FOR YOUR HERO, AND THE BATTLE SEEM UNWINNABLE!

NNNGGH!

NOW... I DESTROY YOU!

CHECK!

YIPES!

I WANTED THAT! WAAAHHH!

YOU ARE NOT MY BEST FRIEND ANY MORE!!

BUT... BUT..

AND JUST WHEN ALL SEEMS LOST...

...THAT'S WHEN YOUR HERO USES ALL THEIR STRENGTH, COURAGE AND RESOURCES...

...AND TURNS IT AROUND!

NO - I DESTROY YOU!

WHAK!

CHECK-MATE!

BOOM!

NOOO!

BUT LOOK! I BAKED YOU A CAKE!

YAY!

AND THAT'S JUST FOR STARTERS!

THERE'S ALL SORTS OF OTHER KINDS OF CONFLICTS- MORAL, PHILOSOPHICAL...

WAK!

...FRYING PAN...

OOK.

ART MONKEY CHALLENGE!

  OOK!*

* HERE ARE TWO CHARACTERS WHO LOOK LIKE THEY'RE NOT GOING TO GET ON. NOW IT'S UP TO YOU TO PUT THEM INTO CONFLICT!

TRY DRAWING YOUR OWN COMIC ABOUT WHAT HAPPENS WHEN THESE GUYS MEET!

USE THE QUESTIONS AT THE BOTTOM TO HELP YOU FIGURE OUT YOUR STORY IF YOU'RE STUCK!

KID LUMBERJACK

 VS

ROBO BEAR

HOW DO THEY MEET?

WHAT ARE THEY FIGHTING OVER?

WHERE IS THIS HAPPENING?

WHAT FORM DOES THEIR CONFLICT TAKE?

WHO WINS?

CHAINSAW FIGHT?

ARGUMENT?

VIDEOGAME CONTEST?

(AWESOME) ENDINGS

1.

SO, TO RECAP: WE'VE TALKED ABOUT ALL THE DIFFERENT THINGS YOU NEED TO MAKE A STORY...

...A HERO...

THE BANK IS BEING ROBBED! HELP US, TRICERACOP!

I'M ON IT, CITIZEN!

GASP! IT'S CRIMINAL MASTERMIND, DOCTOR DIMETRODON!

BANK

BWA HA HA HA HA!

2.

...A BADDY...

3.

...SOME CONFLICT...

I'M TAKING ALL THE GOLD! AND IF YOU TRY AND STOP ME...

I'LL BLOW UP THAT BUS FULL OF ORPHANS!

TNT

4.

...AND NOW IT'S TIME FOR THE FINAL STEP – ENDINGS!

NOW, YOU CAN END A STORY IN ALL SORTS OF WAYS.

USUALLY, PEOPLE LIKE A
HAPPY ENDING

HA! I ATE THE BOMB! YOU'RE UNDER ARREST, DIMETRODON!!

BURRP!

CURSE YOU, TRICERACOP!

EW, HAVE YOU BEEN EATING EGGS?

BUT IT'S UP TO YOU - YOU COULD TRY A
SAD ENDING

SORRY, CHIEF. THE BUS BLEW UP AND DIMETRODON GOT AWAY.

HAND OVER YOUR BADGE AND GUN, TRICERACOP - YOU'RE FIRED!

OR EVEN MIX THINGS UP WITH A SHOCKING
TWIST ENDING!

WAH! I WAS JUST HAVING THE WEIRDEST DREAM!

AH, GO BACK TO SLEEP.

FOR A MORE *MATURE* APPROACH, WHY NOT LEAVE SOME QUESTIONS UNANSWERED, WITH AN
AMBIGUOUS ENDING

DIMETRODON GOT AWAY... I GUESS WE'LL NEVER KNOW WHAT HE REALLY WANTED.

...OR WHO MY REAL FATHER IS!

OR LEAVE YOUR AUDIENCE ON THE *EDGE OF THEIR SEATS* WITH A
CLIFFHANGER ENDING

I'VE DEFUSED THE BOMB - BUT NOW A GIANT METEOR IS ABOUT TO HIT THE EARTH!

AH, NUTS.

TO BE CONTINUED?

ART MONKEY CHALLENGE!

OOK!*

* SEE IF YOU CAN BEAT THOSE, AND THINK UP YOUR OWN ENDING - PUT IT IN THE BLANK PANEL ABOVE!

APPENDIX ALERT
TURN TO PAGE 62

WANT MORE PRACTICE TELLING AWESOME STORIES? APPENDIX G HAS TWO UNFINISHED COMICS FOR YOU TO COMPLETE!

HOW TO MAKE

(...WHICH ARE AWESOME)

HOW TO MAKE **YOUR VERY OWN** COMICS

21:

(WHICH ARE *AWESOME*)

WE'VE LOOKED AT ALL THE DIFFERENT ASPECTS OF MAKING COMICS IN THESE LESSONS...

HOW TO HAVE IDEAS AND MAKE UP *CHARACTERS*...

THING THAT IS AWESOME + THING THAT IS AWESOME

= THING THAT IS **TOTALLY SUPER AWESOME**

HOW TO TURN THOSE IDEAS INTO *STORIES*...

1. GOODY 2. BADDY
3. THEY FIGHT 4. GOODY WINS

...AND, OF COURSE, HOW TO ACTUALLY *DRAW STUFF!*

...AND NOW IT'S TIME TO PUT IT ALL TOGETHER, AND LEARN HOW TO MAKE YOUR *VERY OWN COMIC!*

---

1 THE *TECHNICAL* BIT!

TAKE A PIECE OF PAPER.

FOLD IT IN HALF.

TA-DA! YOU NOW HAVE A BLANK FOUR-PAGE COMIC, JUST WAITING TO BE DRAWN IN!

P1 / P2 P3 / P4

AND IF YOU ADD A SECOND SHEET OF PAPER, YOU CAN MAKE AN EIGHT-PAGE COMIC!

P1 P5 / P1 P3

 3 SHEETS = **12** PAGES
P1 P3 P5

 4 SHEETS = **16** PAGES
P1 P3 P5 P7

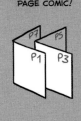
...AND SO ON. FOR EXAMPLE, AN ISSUE OF THE AWESOME PHOENIX COMIC HAS 32 PAGES - 8 SHEETS!

HOWEVER MANY SHEETS YOU USE, JUST REMEMBER: THE ONE ON THE OUTSIDE WILL BE THE FRONT AND BACK COVERS...
BACK COVER / FRONT COVER!

...AND THE ONE IN THE MIDDLE WILL BE THE CENTRE SPREAD - THAT'S A GOOD PLACE FOR POSTERS AND STUFF!
CENTRE SPREAD

---

2 THE *CREATIVE* BIT!

SO FIRST, THINK OF A *NAME* FOR YOUR COMIC...

THE DRAGON
THE ZAP!
THE BUMBO
THE MONKEY

...AND DRAW A LOGO!

NOW, DECIDE WHAT TO PUT IN IT!

SHORT, FUNNY STRIPS?

LONGER, ADVENTURE STORIES?

OR A MIX OF BOTH?

AND WHAT *KIND* OF STORIES?

Sci-fi? COMEDY? Soap Opera? FANTASY?

OR MAYBE EVEN SOME *HISTORY* OR COOL *SCIENCE?*

SERIOUS, SCARY, BONKERS - OR A BIT OF EVERYTHING?!

NEXT: WHO'S GOING TO *MAKE* IT?

ARE YOU GOING TO DO EVERY-THING YOURSELF?

OR WILL YOU BE THE EDITOR, AND GET ALL YOUR FRIENDS TO DRAW STORIES?

---

3 THE *NEXT* BIT!

HOORAY, YOU'VE MADE A COMIC! NOW WHAT DO YOU DO WITH IT?

YOU COULD USE A PHOTOCOPIER OR PRINTER TO MAKE COPIES OF IT!

THEN YOU CAN GIVE COPIES TO YOUR FRIENDS! YOU COULD EVEN *SELL* THEM! YOU'LL BE *RICH!**

*NOTE: YOU MIGHT NOT GET RICH. NOT IMMEDIATELY, ANYWAY.

YOU COULD EVEN PUT YOUR COMICS ON THE *INTERNET!*

JUST THINK, THEN PEOPLE ALL OVER THE WORLD WOULD BE ABLE TO READ *YOUR* COMICS!

THERE'S NOTHING STOPPING YOU! GET GOING! *CONQUER THE WORLD WITH COMICS!*

Panel 1: I AM GOING TO PROVE MY THEORY THAT *ANYONE* CAN MAKE COMICS! / I MEAN, COME ON...

Panel 2: YOU JUST TAKE A SHEET OF PAPER... / FOLD IT IN HALF...

Panel 3: ...AND THEN DRAW COMICS ON IT! / SEE? SUPER EASY! WHY, EVEN *A DOOFUS* COULD DO IT!

Panel 4: AND TO PROVE IT... LET'S *MEET* ONE! / OUR ALL-PURPOSE ASSISTANT, GENERAL LACKEY AND RESIDENT *DOOFUS: NEILL CAMERON!* / UM... HELLO? / WHAT'S THAT YOU'VE GOT THERE, ASSISTANT? / OOK.* / * NICE HAT.

Row 2, Panel 1: THIS IS *SPLAT!* IT'S A COMIC MY BROTHER AND ME MADE WHEN WE WERE KIDS! / LOOK, I'LL SHOW YOU SOME OF THE CHARACTERS!

Panel 2: HERE'S *OLD STINKER!* HE WAS A TALKING COW POO. / EWW! / OOK.* / * WELL, THAT'S JUST DISGUSTING.

Panel 3: AND HERE'S *JOHN JUMP!* / HE COULD JUMP. / O...KAY. / WHEEEE!

Panel 4: THIS IS *SUPER CHEESE SANDWICH MAN!* / HE'S A CHEESE SANDWICH. BUT, Y'KNOW, *SUPER!* / OOK.* / * I LIKE CHEESE SANDWICHES.

Panel 5: AND HERE'S MY FAVOURITE... *THE AMAZING TEABAG!* / LOOK, LET'S READ THE WHOLE THING!

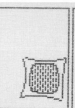

Row 3: The Amazing Teabag / WOW!!! / I'm SO excited / UM... ...I DON'T GET IT. / MAYBE YOU SHOULD GO BACK TO YOUR ASSISTANT-CUPBOARD AND HAVE A NICE LIE DOWN... / I THOUGHT IT WAS FUNNY... / OOK.

Bottom: THINK YOU CAN DO BETTER THAN *TEABAGS* AND *COW POO,* READERS? / OOK!* / * I BET YOU CAN! / THEN WHY NOT TRY OUR FINAL...

ART MONKEY CHALLENGE!

THE SOMETHING

* OKAY, GUYS! YOU ARE READY TO GO! TIME TO TRY MAKING YOUR *VERY OWN COMIC!* / OOK!* / REMEMBER TO GIVE IT A *COVER* AND A *TITLE...* / AND THEN JUST FILL IT WITH *AWESOME ACTION, COMEDY* AND *EXCITEMENT!* / *COMICS GLORY AWAITS!*

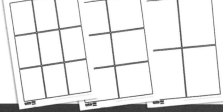

REMEMBER, YOU CAN DOWNLOAD BLANK COMICS PAGES TO GET YOU STARTED, ALONG WITH ALL OF THE ART MONKEY CHALLENGES AT:

www.thephoenixcomic.co.uk/awesome

SUPERCHEESESANDWICHMAN IS.02) JAMES CAMERON. WHO IS A SMELLY MAN

AWESOME
APPENDICES

MORE
(AWESOME)
STUFF

APPENDIX MORE STUFF THAT IS AWESOME

OOK!*

* TRY MIXING AND MATCHING SOME OF THESE INGREDIENTS TO CREATE AWESOME NEW CHARACTERS!

ZOMBIE

MUMMY

VAMPIRE

WEREWOLF

GHOST

KNIGHT

SAMURAI

SPACEMAN

PANDA

DRAGON

WIZARD

WITCH

PENGUIN

BUILDER

WRESTLER

DUCK

COWBOY

PRINCESS

SNOWMAN

SKELETON

MUTANT

MONSTER

DETECTIVE

SUPERHERO

POP STAR

APPENDIX B INVENTORY OF COOL ROBOT ACCESSORIES

TRACKS!

WHEELS

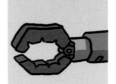

JETS!

COGS!

SHOULDER PADS!

MISSILES!

CLAWS

MORE MISSILES!

VENTS

HEADLIGHTS

SPEAKERS

CHAINSAW

EVEN **MORE** MISSILES!

SINK PLUNGERS!

A NICE PRETTY BOW!

APPENDIX C INVENTORY OF PIRATE MOUSTACHERY

THE "BRIGADIER"

THE "THOMPSON"

THE "FARMER JOE"

THE "COLONEL"

THE "DROOPY"

THE "INSPECTOR"

THE "BOOMERANG"

THE "WHALE TAIL"

THE "ALEX"

THE "CAPTAIN"

THE "POINTY POINTY"

THE "GAFFER"

THE "MAD PROFESSOR"

THE "NEAT 'N' TIDY"

THE "HAIRY EARS"

APPENDIX **D** HOW TO DRAW

DINOSAURS
STEP-BY-STEP

DIPLODOCUS

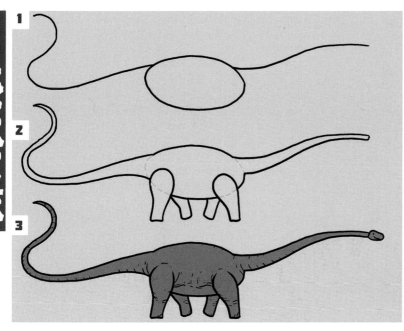

APATOSAURUS

(SAME BASIC SHAPE, BUT SQUATTER, BULKIER)

BRACHIOSAURUS

(TALLER, MORE UPRIGHT)

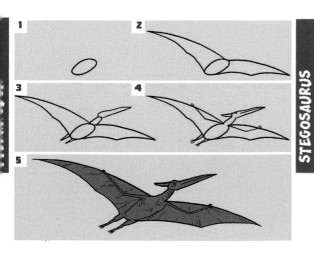

STEGOSAURUS

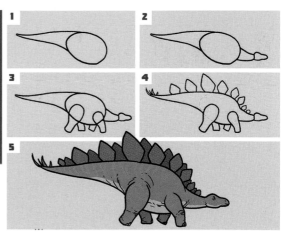

APPENDIX E STEP-BY-STEP CREEPY CREATURES

VAMPIRE

WEREWOLF

ZOMBIE

MUMMY

APPENDIX  STEP-BY-STEP PENGUINS

1

2

3

4

5

6

AWESOME PENGUIN VARIANTS

NINJA

CHEF

SAILOR

MORE FUN COMICS!

EXTRA ART MONKEY CHALLENGE

OOK!

• HERE ARE A COUPLE MORE COMIC STRIPS FOR YOU TO FINISH OFF!

THE GNARLED STUMP, A DISTINCTLY DISREPUTABLE WATERING HOLE WHERE PIRATES GATHER TO DRINK AND DO WHAT PIRATES LIKE BEST...

... ARGUE ABOUT WHO IS THE BEST PIRATE!

YARRR!! I BE THE BEST PIRATE OF ALL!

A SHARK TOOK ME HAND, AN' NOW I'VE GOT A HOOK!

A HOOK? YARRR, THAT'S NOTHING! A CROCODILE TOOK MY HAND, AND NOW I'VE GOT A _____!

YARRR, SISSY STUFF! A SHOAL OF PIRANHAS TOOK ME WHOLE ARM, AND I REPLACED IT WITH... _____!

HA! YER ALL SISSIES! A GANG OF ANGRY DONKEYS BIT OFF BOTH ME ARMS AND BOTH ME LEGS...

...AND I REPLACED 'EM WITH... _____!

SO, AM I THE WINNER?

YOU CERTAINLY ARRRRRRR!

THE END!

IT WAS THE DAY *TERROR* CAME TO OUR WORLD! LANDMARKS *FELL* AND NATIONS *TREMBLED*, AS PLANET EARTH FACED...

THE INVASION OF THE !

...BOARD THE ALIEN MOTHERSHIP...

HA HA HA! THE PUNY HUMANS CANNOT MATCH THE POWER OF OUR -RAYS!

HA HA HA! THEY ARE PUNY!

SEND IN THE ARMY!

10

WE *DID*, PRIME MINISTER! THEY GOT CREAMED!

UM, THE NAVY?

THEM TOO!

WELL, NUTS.

IT'S OKAY - WE JUST GOT A MESSAGE! THE ALIENS ALL DIED OF !

HOORAY!

THE END!

OOK!*

* SOMETHING IS CHASING PROF. P, ART MONKEY AND THEIR PALS – BUT WHAT?

USE ALL YOUR AWESOME ARTISTIC ABILITIES TO FINISH THE DRAWING!